Green Treefrog Care

For Jenny

Quick & Easy Green Treefrog Care

Project Team
Editor: Tom Mazorlig
Copy Editor: Carl Schutt
Design: Patricia Escabi
Series Design: Mary Ann Kahn

T.F.H. Publications
President/CEO: Glen S. Axelrod
Executive Vice President: Mark E. Johnson
Publisher: Christopher T. Reggio
Production Manager: Kathy Bontz

T.F.H. Publications, Inc.
One TFH Plaza
Third and Union Avenues
Neptune City, NJ 07753

Library of Congress Cataloging-in-Publication Data
Purser, Phillip.
Quick and easy green treefrog care / Phillip Purser.
p. cm.
Includes index.
ISBN 0-7938-1024-8 (alk. paper)
    1.   Green treefrogs as pets. I. Title.
SF459.F83P87 2005
639.3'7878—dc22
2005004684

This book has been published with the intent to provide accurate and authoritative information in regard to the subject matter within. While every precaution has been taken in preparation of this book, the author and publisher expressly disclaim responsibility for any errors, omissions, or adverse effects arising from the use or application of the information contained herein. The techniques and suggestions are used at the reader's discretion and are not to be considered a substitute for veterinary care. If you suspect a medical problem, consult your veterinarian.

The Leader In Responsible Animal Care For Over 50 Years!™
www.tfhpublications.com

Table
of Contents

Meet the Green Treefrog

A beautifully colored animal, the green treefrog is a benign, pleasant creature that, because of his hardy constitution, healthy appetite, and inherent beauty, makes an excellent amphibian to keep in captivity. After nearly a quarter century of keeping and studying reptiles and amphibians, I still have a soft spot in my heart for the vibrant shades and haunting songs of these emerald-hued treefrogs. With their slightly upturned mouths and wide-open eyes, the green treefrogs seem to be wearing a perpetual smile. A wonderful animal all around!

But enough about my affections for the treefrogs; if you're reading this book, you obviously have an interest in the treefrogs,

Scientific Names

You may have noticed that sometimes there are words in italics that appear after the name of an animal. This is the scientific name, and each animal only has one scientific name. Biologists determine the scientific name of each animal based on what other animals he is related to. The first part of the name is called the *genus* (plural: *genera*). The second part is the *species*, and this combination of genus and species is unique for each animal.

The reason scientific names exist is so that scientists all over the world can talk about each animal without worrying about language barriers or other similar animals being confused with the one they want to discuss. For example, there are many green treefrogs, but only the small greenish treefrog of eastern North America is called *Hyla cinerea*.

If you use the genus name once, you can abbreviate it to the first letter when you write about it later. So, if I were talking about green treefrogs again, I could just type *H. cinerea*. Also, if I wanted to talk about all the treefrogs in the same genus as the green treefrog, I would just say *Hyla*.

It's a good idea to become accustomed to scientific names, since hobbyists and writers use them frequently.

particularly the green treefrog, and you want to know more about them.

Green Treefrogs in Nature

Green treefrogs are small amphibians (a group of animals that have gilled aquatic larvae and air-breathing adults) belonging to the family Hylidae, which boasts over 640 species divided between 37 genera worldwide. Within the genus *Hyla* alone there are more than 250 species of treefrogs found throughout North America, South America,

Quick & Easy Green Treefrog Care

Europe, Asia, and Africa. The diversity among these species is truly amazing, and the hobbyist interested in keeping treefrogs certainly has a vast selection from which to choose.

First appearing in the fossil record over 120 million years ago, the treefrogs of the genus *Hyla* are highly advanced creatures whose bodies have specially evolved for life in the forest canopy. Like all treefrogs, the green treefrog's toes have evolved into broad, flat, sticky pads that can cling to virtually any surface. These

As their name suggests, green treefrogs are arboreal animals, spending most of their time in the branches of trees and shrubs.

modified toes—coupled with the animal's dexterous limbs and light-weight body—allow the green treefrog to climb high into the treetops or jump from leaf to leaf without falling.

Speaking of jumping, green treefrogs have long hind legs that are strapped with powerful muscles. When startled or in pursuit of prey, a green treefrog can leap over ten times his own body length. That's the equivalent of a six-foot tall man leaping the length of two school buses!

Clad in emerald to olive green with yellow to golden stripes running from the corner of the mouth along the animal's flanks, the green treefrog may also sport golden speckles over its head and back, making it one of the more aesthetically attractive treefrogs available in the pet trade today. With all that green and yellow on his body, it's easy to see how the green treefrog can stay so camouflaged in the wild. His back is bright green so that any birds looking down for a meal will not be able to discern the green of the frog from the green of the leaves. Similarly, the green treefrog's belly is pale whitish to yellow, helping the frog to

Herp is the Word

Throughout this book, you will see the term *herps*. This word refers both to reptiles and amphibians and comes from the word *herpetology*, which is the study of these two groups of animals. When speaking of the hobby of keeping reptiles and amphibians, you can call it the *herp hobby*. *Herpetoculture* is the keeping and breeding of reptiles and amphibians. A *herper* is some one who participates in the herp hobby or herpetoculture.

blend almost perfectly with the sun-dappled understory. Any snakes, perched birds, weasels, or other ground-going predators will very often overlook the green treefrog when glancing up at him from the forest floor.

Nocturnal animals, green treefrogs are primarily active in the hours from twilight to well after midnight, but return to the safety of the canopy several hours before dawn. Green treefrogs have no trouble seeing in the dark and can navigate and hunt with ease in the black of night. Highly vocal animals, the green treefrogs have a unique system of trills and calls that they use to communicate with other treefrogs. Communication is especially notable during the mating season (when males will call to attract mates), but calling can also be used as a sort of alarm when predators are near. Under normal circumstances, a green treefrog may sing or chorus in the company of others of his kind. When a predator draws near, however, the frogs nearest to it fall silent. Their sudden silence acts as a warning to all nearby green treefrogs that danger is at hand. When the predator has moved on, the frogs will resume their chorusing.

Green Treefrogs Sources

The good news for amphibian hobbyists is that green treefrogs and their kin are some of the easiest of all frogs to care for in captivity. Young herp enthusiasts and beginning treefrog keepers are encouraged to start off with a green treefrog (or two) before moving on to some of the more difficult species. Because of their benevolent disposition and communal nature, green treefrogs may be kept in pairs, trios, or even larger colonies depending on how much time and space the hobbyist can dedicate to his or her frogs. When kept under suitable conditions, green treefrogs can live for a surprisingly long time. The captive average life span is two to four years, with life spans of five or six years not uncommon.

Because they are so common in the pet trade, green treefrogs may be acquired from a variety of sources. Local pet shops specializing in reptiles and amphibians are likely to carry green treefrogs, as well as a host of other treefrogs. Buying from a pet shop is usually your best option, as the shopkeeper will likely have several animals to choose from. In a pet shop, you can view and inspect any treefrog before making a purchase.

Ordering a green treefrog from a reputable online dealer is another viable option. The only major drawbacks to ordering your green treefrogs online are your inability to inspect the frogs before making purchase and the exorbitant cost of shipping. Since overnight shipping is costly, you'll likely spend a lot more on shipping fees than you will on your treefrog.

A final option for green treefrog acquisition is to catch your own from the wild. If you live within the green treefrog's natural geographic range, taking a slow drive down some lonely asphalt roads on warm, rainy nights is a surefire way of finding some green treefrogs.

State Amphibian

In the spring of 2005, the state government of Georgia—the author's home state—recognized the popularity of the green treefrog by naming him the state amphibian.

Many dealers overcrowd their green treefrogs, which promotes the spread of disease among the animals. Try to find a source that provides better housing for the frogs.

Appearing as golden-green lumps perched atop the asphalt, these frogs will take great, gangly leaps at your approach and may be difficult to catch at first. Once you get the hang of it, catching some green treefrogs will become easier. The only disadvantages to capturing your own green treefrogs from the wild are that these animals are protected by law in some areas. Make sure to check all state and local laws regarding wildlife collection before you plan on capturing any wild green treefrogs.

Selection

As I previously mentioned, purchasing your green treefrogs from a retail pet dealer is probably your best bet, as you can view and inspect your choice before buying it. Viewing and inspecting a green treefrog before making purchase is a critical step in selecting a healthy animal. To ensure a successful green treefrog keeping endeavor, your chosen specimen should meet or surpass the criteria outlined below.

Treefrogs are naturally arboreal. Healthy individuals should be clinging to the glass, limbs, plants, or other structures near the top of the terrarium. Avoid purchasing individuals that are on the ground or floor of the terrarium, as they are likely unhealthy. (The exception to

Obey the Law

this rule comes when the top of the tank is too hot, causing all treefrogs to retreat to the bottom of the terrarium in search of cooler temperatures).

The green treefrogs's body should be uniformly colored and textured: pale spots, patches of discoloration, sores, lesions, redness about the legs or belly, or clouded eyes are definite signs of poor health.

Healthy frogs should have a rounded appearance. A protruding backbone or pronounced hips or pelvic girdle are signs that the treefrog is underweight or malnourished. The pronounced outline of the bones of the skull is another indicator that the treefrog is not eating enough.

When picked up, your treefrog should exhibit definite signs of vitality. A healthy individual will kick, jump, perch, walk, or otherwise move about in your hands. His eyes will be wide open and he may even call or cry out when touched. Healthy specimens will never appear weak, lethargic, limp, or otherwise immobile.

Watch your chosen treefrog feed. Healthy specimens will attack their prey with great enthusiasm, leaping from their perch with mouth wide open and

The barking treefrog is another hardy, common, and inexpensive treefrog that is easy and fun to keep.

gobbling up their food while it is still alive! Animals that do not display such gusto during feeding time are likely ill and may never feed properly again. If possible, check your chosen treefrog's feces, which should be dark and solid. Runny or bloody stool is an indicator of that frog harboring internal parasites. Never purchase such an animal.

If the treefrog you have selected has satisfied all these criteria, then you've likely found a very healthy animal, indeed. Once you make your purchase, it's best to transport your new friend home in an opaque container, such as a deli cup or small box. Transporting your treefrog in a clear container will stress the animal, as he will see and hear all the commotion around him and, because he is in a clear container, he will try to escape. Jumping and leaping repeatedly into the walls of a clear container can cause injury to your pet. A treefrog that is transported in an opaque container will nestle snugly into one corner and quietly weather the journey home. If you are purchasing your treefrog in the hot summertime, or if you have a long drive ahead of you, place a moist paper towel in the bottom of the container, and keep the container in a cool place within your vehicle and out of direct sunlight.

Before you ever consider making a purchase, however, you need to have an established terrarium or vivarium waiting at home to receive your new pet. Making a smooth transition from pet shop to home terrarium is a critical step in ensuring a long, successful endeavor with your treefrog. The longer your treefrog has to sit and wait in his transportation container, the more likely he will stress or even take ill.

The Treefrog Terrarium

One of the best practical aspects about keeping green treefrogs as pets is their limited need for space. A single green treefrog may be adequately housed in a 10-gallon terrarium sitting atop a desk, end table, or even on a shelf in your office. Green treefogs simply are not roaming animals. Even in the wild a treefrog is content to sit and watch the world go by from the branches of a single tree for season after season, so long as food and water are abundant. Housing, at least so far as size goes, is largely up to you, for it makes no difference to the frogs. If housing multiple green treefrogs, however, you should not house them any more densely than one frog per ten gallons of living space.

Quarantine

There are two types of terraria to construct for your green treefrogs. The first is the quarantine tank. Also known as the hospital tank, the quarantine terrarium will be the home of your new green treefrog for the first few weeks. The quarantine period is a time to watch your new pet and to observe him for any signs of illness before bringing your newest treefrog into contact with the rest of your reptile and amphibian collection. By isolating your new green treefrog from the rest of your herps, you can ensure that any communicable diseases the new frog has will not spread and infect your other pets. It is best to establish your quarantine tank in another room of your house, preferably as far away from any other herps as possible.

Because of your need to closely observe your new green treefrog, his quarantine enclosure must be sparsely furnished. Dense vegetation that would allow your green treefrog to vanish from sight has no place in the quarantine terrarium. Construct a quarantine tank by placing several layers of paper towels on the floor of an all-glass

Quarantine your new treefrog in a simple cage for at least 14 days and observe him for signs of illness before you move him into his permanent home.

aquarium. Do not use paper towels that have dyes or prints in them. Many of these dyes contain harmful chemicals that can soak through your treefrog's skin and cause discomfort or illness. Solid white paper towels also provide an excellent, high-contrast background for your green treefrog's droppings, giving you the chance to inspect your new pet's stool for consistency and color (healthy stool is soft, but solid, and is dark brown to black).

To satisfy your green treefrog's need for moisture and humidity, place a large plastic dish in the bottom of the quarantine terrarium, filled about two inches deep with clean, fresh water. Into this dish of water you should run a length of PVC pipe that is long enough to prop at an angle in the terrarium. This length of pipe will act as a "haul-out," or escape route should your treefrog fall into the water. This pipe will also function as a perch for your treefrog during its stay in quarantine.

Attach an adhering-style thermometer and humidity gauge (both of which can be obtained at your local pet shop) on the glass in the center of the quarantine terrarium. Placing these gauges too close to the top or bottom of the terrarium might skew their readings. Temperature should range in the mid-70s (Fahrenheit), while relative humidity should range between 60 and 70 percent. The good news is that the green treefrog's preferred temperature is much the same as our own preferred temperature, so whatever room temperature your home sustains is likely sufficient for your treefrog. If, however, you need additional heat in your treefrog's enclosure, you might want to place a fully submersible aquarium heater into a deep plastic storage container filled with water. Cover the container with a perforated lid, leaving enough room for the cord of the heater to run out, but not enough room for your treefrog to crawl inside. Set the heater at 77 to 78°F and plug it in. As the heater gently warms the water inside the covered container, warm, moist air will escape into the terrarium, thereby raising the temperature and humidity levels inside quarantine.

Buying the Right Thermometer

You need to have an accurate thermometer for your green treefrog terrarium. The most accurate thermometers are digital ones. You can get one at an electronics store or home improvement store; they are not normally sold at pet stores. Mercury bulb thermometers (nowadays not usually filled with mercury) and dial-face thermometers are reasonably accurate. The thin strips that stick on the glass are not.

Because green treefrogs are sensitive to excessive moisture (relative humidity above 85 percent is considered saturated, and is highly detrimental to many species of treefrog), it is important that your quarantine terrarium receive plenty of ventilation. Using a fine-mesh screen lid will allow for sufficient entry of fresh oxygen, while at the same time aiding in the release of excess humidity, carbon dioxide, and nitrogenous gases (namely ammonia) from the terrarium. It is critical that you *never use a glass lid on your treefrog terrarium*. Glass lids allow for no airflow, so no fresh oxygen can enter the tank. A glass lid will also lock in humidity and the noxious gases associated with your treefrog's wastes, making for a stagnant, unhealthy atmosphere in the terrarium.

If, after a period of at least 14 days of close observation, your green treefrog has shown no symptoms of disease or illness, you may bring him into his permanent terrarium. If you already have an established terrarium with other treefrogs, then after a 14-day quarantine period, you may introduce your new treefrog into the communal terrarium.

Permanent Housing

When it comes to constructing the permanent terrarium where your green treefrogs will live, you have many options. Green treefrogs are highly adaptable animals who can adjust to life in a great many environs. Some green treefrogs, for example, may live their entire lives in the canopy and understory of a live oak grove in southern Georgia. Others might be perfectly at home living in a nook under a gutter awning in an industrial park in eastern Texas, venturing out only at night to feed and spawn. The point is that the style of terrarium you construct is largely up to your own tastes and desires, just so long as the terrarium meets your green treefrog's needs for humidity, air circulation, and temperature.

If you opt for a less intricate terrarium that is easier to clean and maintain, you will gain ground in the "duty and work" department, but this ease of maintenance will come at the cost of aesthetics. Use an all-glass aquarium of at least the 10-gallon (preferably 20-gallon) size. Do not use wooden enclosures, as the grain of the wood will harbor molds, bacteria, and fungi that can prove dangerous to your treefrog. In the bottom of the glass aquarium, place several layers of white or plain paper towels. Atop this substrate, place a water dish and length of PVC as described for the quarantine terrarium. Now you may be wondering what is the difference between this terrarium and the quarantine tank? Simple. It's the vegetation! Once you have the PVC (or several lengths of PVC) in place, you will want to put some artificial plants throughout the terrarium. Although there are limitless varieties of plastic, silk, and other artificial plants on the market, I highly recommend those plastic types that adhere to the glass of the tank by way of suction cups. This style of plant comes

Ventilation

While humidity is important, you must not forget about air circulation. Outfit your treefrog's terrarium with a screen or mesh lid so that fresh oxygen can enter the tank and noxious gases can escape. If the humidity is too low, you can cover one-third of the screen with a piece of plastic or glass to lessen the evaporation. Do not cover more than one-third, or the ventilation will be insufficient.

in a variety of realistic types (ferns, vines, broad-leafed, etc.) and can be utilized at any level of the tank. Placed on the floor, the plants will act as ground cover. Placed on the walls of the tank, the plants will make great perches while your treefrog roams about. Hung high in the terrarium, these artificial plants will make an excellent canopy in which your green treefrog will take refuge during the day. Because these plants are plastic, they are easily washed clean.

When it comes time to clean this style of terrarium, you need only remove the treefrog to a holding tank or container, dispose of the substrate, and wash the terrarium, water dishes, PVC pipes, and plastic plants in a bath of hot, soapy water. Dishwashing soaps work well for this purpose because they are antibacterial and rinse completely away. Do not wash any item in the treefrog terrarium with harsh cleansers, especially pine-scented varieties. The silicon that cements the walls of the terrarium is a highly porous material that may retain trace amounts of these chemicals. Since your green treefrog may spend most of his days perched quietly atop the silicon seam of the terrarium, any remaining amounts of harsh cleanser could easily soak through his skin and prove fatal. After washing them thoroughly with a mild soap, rinse and dry all materials, and replace them atop a fresh layer of white paper towel substrate. Now return your treefrog to his freshly cleaned home. It's just that easy!

No matter what species of treefrog you keep (a Cuban treefrog is pictured here), a wooden terrarium is not recommended, as it will harbor mold.

The Naturalistic Terrarium

The second type of home terrarium is the natural terrarium, or vivarium, which incorporates a wide variety of natural elements in its construction. They are living, breathing mini-ecosystems.

Reminder: Rinse Well

When cleaning your treefrog's enclosure, you must rinse thoroughly. Any traces of soap can harm your frog. Remember to rinse all parts of the decorations, the water bowl, and the thermometer.

These elaborate enclosures may contain permanent pools, waterfalls, rivulets, and an assortment of live mosses, ferns, and broad-leaf plants. Some terrariums even have deep pools containing fish, tadpoles, newts, and other benign creatures. Natural terrariums require lots of planning and maintenance, and they are certainly not for everyone. Before embarking on such an entailed project, the hobbyist must ponder some realistic questions. Do I have the time and resources it takes to maintain a living terrarium? Is this style of terrarium best for my chosen species of treefrog?

If a naturalistic terrarium is right for you, then there are a thousand different directions you might go in, and there are hundreds of plant/fern/water combinations to choose from. Below, however, is a generic how-to guide for constructing the foundation of a living, breathing terrarium.

Begin by pouring a two-inch deep layer of aquarium pebbles into the tank. With your hand, sweep a section of the terrarium floor free of the pebbles. Edge this area with larger, smooth stones to prevent the smaller pebbles from shifting and sliding back into the clearing. This area will become a pool in time. Now place an inch or two of peat moss atop the gravel, again leaving the swept-clean area open to become a pool. Over the peat, place a layer of moist, living green moss. This moss-peat-pebble construct will act as the substrate and will be the medium in which your living plants will root.

Any one of the following plants makes an excellent addition to the living green treefrog terrarium: English ivy, Chinese evergreen, arrowhead, philodendron, pothos, and bromeliads, or "air-plants," which have no root system. If you have a large pool of water in your vivarium, you can add some water hyacinth, which is not only attractive, but also serves to clean your terrarium's water table by filtering out biological wastes through its roots. There are numerous other species of plants that would be appropriate. A search of the Internet will reveal dozens of choices.

To insert a plant into your terrarium, simply poke a hole through the substrate with your finger until you touch the glass of the terrarium floor. Gently place the roots of each plant into the depression, and push the pebbles/peat over the roots. Add water by gently pouring water into the cleared pool section of the tank. Add enough water such that the pool is full, but the land is still dry. If your substrate is three inches deep, for example, you should add water until it reaches the two and three-quarters inch mark. This will ensure that sufficient water reaches the roots of your plants, while at the same time giving your green treefrog plenty of dry land to roam on. Remember, the evaporating water from the pool will provide plenty of humidity, so there is no need to keep the substrate saturated.

Misting your vivarium should be a daily practice. To ensure the proper growth of the plants and health of your treefrog(s), you'll want to spray a gentle mist over everything within the terrarium each morning. This fine mist (sprayed with a hand-held misting bottle or garden sprayer) will not only stimulate and refresh the plant's leaves and your treefrog's skin, but it will also help to wash away any filth or debris which may have accumulated from the previous day. Misting is especially important in vivariums containing mosses, lichens, and bromeliads, all of which have shallow running roots or no roots at all. In order to survive, these plants must be misted daily. Take care not to overmist your vivarium, however, as too much moisture is definitely a bad thing. Misting the vivarium once a day usually is sufficient.

Prepping the Plants

Most houseplants have been treated with an array of pesticides, fertilizers, and other nasty chemicals that might harm your treefrogs. To avoid exposing your frogs to these hazards, wash the plants off before placing them in the terrarium. Remove each plant from its pot, rinse all the dirt off the roots, wash the leaves with mild soapy water, and rinse thoroughly (note that sometimes plants die after this procedure, but most will bounce back). If you are going to put the plant in a pot in the terrarium, repot the plant in a clean pot with organic potted soil. Bury the pot in the substrate to hide it.

If your terrarium contains pools that are deep enough to accommodate one, you might want to include a fully submersible filter into your miniature bio-scape. Fitted with activated carbon and filtration media, these filters not only help to remove ammonia and nitrogenous wastes from the water column, but their suction and expulsion of water helps to keep the entire water column circulating, thereby cutting down on the risk of stagnation and the growth of molds and bacteria in some parts of the terrarium. If your terrarium will accommodate one, I highly recommend using a fully submersible filter.

You can also take a lot of hassle out of cleaning your terrarium by leaving algae on the rocks and substrate of the terrarium, and by rooting plenty of living plants directly into the substrate and water column. As the plants grow and flourish, their root systems will remove ammonia, nitrogen, and other such pollutants from the soil and water. A heavily planted terrarium, therefore, will not only make the habitat much healthier, but it will also require far less maintenance at cleaning time. Lots of plants also cut down on offensive odors by processing the nitrogenous wastes in the soil and water while adding humidity and stimulating air circulation inside

When selecting plants for the terrarium, choose broad-leafed varieties that will give your green treefrogs surfaces to perch on.

the terrarium via photosynthesis. Perhaps the best plant to add to your terrarium is water hyacinth. This plant's ability to process and remove wastes from the water column is nothing short of miraculous, and keeping one or more in your terrarium pools will add both beauty and ecological balance to your green treefrog's habitat.

Maintenance

As you might imagine, cleaning a living, breathing vivarium is very different than cleaning a low-maintenance style terrarium. Clean by removing any visible waste/feces from the glass and surface of the leaves. Wiping the glass with a damp paper towel will also remove any algae that may be obscuring the view. Siphon the water from the pool using an aquarium siphon or a wet/dry shop vacuum. Remember to remove any residents from the vivarium before vacuuming! As you siphon the pool, the rest of the water (carrying with it any dissolved biological wastes) will drain from the substrate and into the pool to be siphoned out. Once you've siphoned out all the water, swab the glass at the bottom of the pool to remove any remaining debris or slime, and replace the water by pouring clean, fresh water into the pool, not through the substrate.

Use only bottled water or purified drinking water. Tap water containing chlorine, fluorine, or other chemicals should be aged in a pitcher or open container for at least 24 hours before adding it to the terrarium. Chlorine and fluorine are gases that, as the water sits out, will dissipate into the atmosphere. Adding chemical-laden water directly into the terrarium is seriously detrimental to your treefrogs. Prolonged exposure to chlorine will very likely prove toxic, if not fatal, to a green treefrog. Once the water is replaced and the vivarium successfully cleaned, you may replace your green treefrogs to their naturalistic habitat.

Lighting

The question of lighting often comes up when housing reptiles and amphibians. While most species of herps do require some type of special lighting or ultraviolet light (UV) exposure, green treefrogs do not have such requirements. Being nocturnal animals, treefrogs are rarely exposed to sunlight; thus, they rarely receive any UV radiation. Some experts in the field disagree, however, and suggest that in order to maintain proper skeletal, muscular, and metabolic growth, treefrogs should receive five to six hours of full-spectrum florescent lighting every day. By using a full-spectrum florescent light bulb between five to seven hours each day, you can provide plenty of light for any living plants in your terrarium and your green treefrogs, too. For a naturalistic enclosure with many plants, you should probably have two to four full-spectrum lights in place.

Alternate lighting sources may be 25-watt red bulbs. Designed specifically for use in reptile and amphibian enclosures, these bulbs will grant your treefrog both light and gentle warmth.

Whatever style of light fixture you use with your green treefrog terrarium, make sure that neither the light, nor the heat generated by the bulb is too intense. Very bright lights will stress your naturally secretive green treefrog, and excessively high temperatures can easily dry your frog out or cook him alive. Signs that the

Because of their size and delicate skin, most treefrogs should not be handled. It is especially easy to injury small species, like squirrel treefrogs.

lighting apparatus is too hot include dry skin, the treefrog seeking shelter on the floor of the terrarium, or even trying to burrow into the substrate to escape the heat. In severe cases, the skin of the green treefrog may take on a reddish-brown coloration, indicative of heat stress. If you notice any of these symptoms in your treefrog, switch to a lower wattage bulb or move your fixture further away from the terrarium. Because green treefrogs like to hide in small, tight places, you must make sure that your frog cannot come into direct contact with the lighting fixture. If your treefrog should be nestled against the bulb when you turn on your light fixture, the resulting burns would be excruciatingly painful to your treefrog and could easily prove fatal. Another advantage of a screen lid acting as a barrier between your treefrog and the lighting apparatus is that it will prevent this scenario from happening.

Handling

Bear in mind that green treefrogs, like most treefrog species, are not very handle-friendly pets. Their semi-permeable and easily torn skin is highly sensitive to chemical toxicity (i.e., your perfume, cologne, or fingernail polish could be detrimental to the animal) and temperature fluctuations (your body heat will quickly raise the blood temperature of a treefrog sitting in your palm). Handling green treefrogs should be a very limited practice, restricted perhaps to periods of transportation, moving the frog from one terrarium to the next, inspecting the animal for injuries or health problems, etc. As attractive as these little amphibians are, they are far more suited to observation and visual study than they are to handling and petting.

Quick & Easy Green Treefrog Care

Feeding Your Treefrogs

Green treefrogs, like all other frogs, are carnivores. More specifically, they are insectivores, meaning that they only consume insects and other small invertebrates. In the wild, these frogs hunt at night, preying upon whatever invertebrates may be unfortunate enough cross their paths: moths, crickets, spiders, caterpillars, flies, roaches, etc. In the captive environment, however, it is virtually impossible to simulate the wide variety of fare that a wild treefrog would normally consume. A good captive diet might consist of a variety of:

- Crickets
- Maggots (Fly Larvae)

- Mealworms
- Wax Worms

Crickets

Crickets should comprise the staple fare of your green treefrog's diet. These protein-rich insects can be purchased from most pet shops, bait shops, and in bulk from mail order or online suppliers. Crickets come in a variety of sizes to accommodate the specific needs of your pet: pinhead (less than one-quarter inch long), week old (slightly larger, often called one-quarters, as in one-quarter grown), two week old (larger still, often called halves), three week old (often called three-quarters) and adult. Recently metamorphosed green treefrogs are still quite small and will require food that is appropriately sized. If you are unsure as to what size of cricket to feed to your treefrog, a good rule of thumb is to feed crickets that are no longer than the length of the frog's head, as measured from nose-tip to the tympanum (eardrum).

A word of caution when feeding crickets to your treefrogs: Crickets are ravenous omnivores, eating anything they can sink their mandibles into, including your treefrog if he cannot escape or

Whether you have a tiny green treefrog or a huge Cuban treefrog, never feed your frog prey that is bigger than his head.

retreat. I have seen more than one green treefrog fatally mangled by a horde of hungry crickets. If you place a large number of crickets (or excessively large crickets) in the terrarium with your treefrog, be sure to avoid a prey-turned-predator scenario by placing several hunks of cut orange or potato in the terrarium as well. These cut edibles will provide food and water for the crickets, thus preventing the crickets from nibbling on your green treefrog.

Not Picky Eaters

Some animals are adapted to eat only one type of food or to exist on a narrow range of foods. Extreme examples that most people are familiar with are the anteaters. They exist solely on ants and termites. Green treefrogs and most other treefrogs do not specialize on any one particular food. They will attempt to catch and consume any creature that is small enough for them to subdue and cram in their mouths. Mostly this means insects, arachnids, and other invertebrates. Larger treefrogs, like the Cuban treefrog, may occasionally eat small lizards, smaller frogs, baby birds, and small mammals. For the most part, treefrogs aren't picky about their prey.

Flies and Larvae

Feeding flies and maggots to your green treefrog is not nearly as disgusting as it sounds. Available by mail order and from online retailers, bulk cups of maggots provide excellent nutrients for small green treefrogs at a low cost. Simply place a shallow dish in the bottom of your treefrog's terrarium, and put several maggots in the dish. Your green treefrog will find the wriggling, writhing motions of the maggots irresistible, and will not hesitate to feed eagerly on these minute munchies. Of course, the maggots will soon pupate and transform into adult flies. Unless there are holes in your terrarium through which the flies can escape, this metamorphosis should not present any problems, for green treefrogs relish adult flies almost as much as the larval (maggot) form.

A Feeding Caution

Crickets and mealworms have sharp, powerful mandibles that can chew through your treefrog's flesh. Remember to never overwhelm your pet by placing too many food items in his terrarium, and do not feed insects that are too large. Doing so could cost your treefrog his life.

A type of housefly with stunted wings is sometimes available. They are sometimes sold under the name of "bungee bugs." If you are worried about flies escaping into your home, you should try to locate this variety. Most pet stores don't carry bungee bugs, but searching online should turn up a source.

Mealworms

When feeding mealworms and superworms to your green treefrog, care must be taken in selecting the size of the food items. Small frogs may not be able to consume large worms (the so-called superworms, kingworms, or king mealworms). Smaller or weaker frogs also risk serious injury from the largest mealworms. Mealworms are actually beetle larvae, and possess strong, sharp mandibles designed for chewing through very tough foods. When attacked by a treefrog, a mealworm will defend itself by biting repeatedly. Because larger mealworms have more powerful defenses, it is better to feed a larger quantity of small mealworms than to risk injury to a smaller treefrog by offering superworms. A steep-sided dish from which the mealworms cannot escape can be placed in the terrarium and filled with a half dozen or so mealworms. Once your green treefrog discovers the mealworms, he will quickly move in for the kill.

Mealworms must not be allowed to roam freely through your terrarium, as they are burrowing creatures by nature, and will quickly disappear under the terrarium's substrate. Like maggots, mealworms will eventually pupate and metamorphose, the adults emerging as small, reddish brown beetles. And, like flies, these beetles will be greedily consumed by a hungry green treefrog. Mealworms of all sizes may be purchased at most pet shops or ordered from online retailers. Storing your mealworms in deli cups at 45 to $50°$F will greatly slow their metamorphosis process, giving them a much longer shelf life.

Two Different Mealworms

Superworms are actually a different species from the small common mealworm. The common mealworm is the larvae of the darkling beetle, and it is a pest of granaries. The superworm is the larvae of a larger tropical beetle. This beetle lays eggs in rotting wood, and the larva—the superworm—burrows through the wood and feeds on it. Superworms are much larger and have stronger jaws than common mealworms. They also are more digestible, so if your frog is big enough to eat superworms, they are an excellent food.

Wax Worms

A final type of worm that your green treefrog will find delightful is the wax worm. Soft, plump, and virtually defenseless, wax worms make an excellent food choice for weak or ailing treefrogs, as well as for the hale and hearty specimens. Wax worms are actually the caterpillar stage of the wax wing moth, and—you guessed it—they are just as edible to the treefrog in moth form as they are in worm form. Offer wax worms in a shallow bowl or dish placed on the floor of the terrarium. Very personable treefrogs may even take wriggling wax worms directly from their keeper's fingers! Wax worms are high in fat and low in most other nutrients. They are best offered occasionally and fed to underweight frogs.

Varied Diet

While each of these insects has its pros and cons so far as nutrition

Tempting Treats

Sometimes when a treefrog is ill or just adapting to captivity, he may refuse food. Try to offer a variety of prey at this time, and see if something tempts your little guy. When all else fails, try feeding wax worms to your treefrog. These pale, plump larvae are soft, juicy, and delicious, and even a hesitant treefrog will rarely refuse such a tasty meal. Another tempting item is the Cuban green roach, which can be purchased through online suppliers.

goes, a mixed diet containing a variety of each of these insects is recommended to maintain a happy, healthy green treefrog. Not only is feeding the same item over and over not nutritious for your frog, it is also boring. Green treefrogs, by instinct, will seek out a variety of prey items, and we as keepers should do everything we can to give them that variety. A hodgepodge of prey will keep our treefrogs in peak physical and mental health. You can also offer other commercially available insects. With some hunting around the Internet, you may be able to find trevo worms, silkworms, tomato worms, and a variety of small roaches.

Feeding the Food

Feeding a diet of exclusively commercially raised insects is not the most nutritious menu in the world. In fact, wild insects may possess many times the amount of vitamins, minerals, and proteins found in farm-raised insects. So how does the hobbyist get all those missing nutrients back? The answer is simple. After purchasing your feeder items, be they crickets, mealworms, or wax worms, place them in a separate container, such as a small aquarium or plastic animal carrier. Fill the floor of their enclosure with fish flakes or crushed fish pellets. Fish food is highly nutritious and contains far more protein than does corn meal or some other grain on which your feeders were previously raised. For crickets, be sure to add pieces of nutritious fruit or vegetable (orange, sweet potato, carrot, collard greens, dandelions, and kale are some of the best choices) to provide moisture and some added nutrients.

Leave the prey items in the container for 24 to 48 hours. During this time, they will feed on the nutrient-rich flakes, and, when your treefrog eats the feeder, all those nutrients will be passed on to your pet amphibian. Sometimes known as gut-loading, this approach of feeding excellent food to your feeder items is a sound practice that will greatly enhance your treefrog's appearance, metabolism, color, skin tone, immune system, and overall health.

Supplements

While a great many reptiles and amphibians require additional vitamin/mineral supplements with their diet, the treefrogs are very delicate when it comes to this matter. Treefrogs that do not receive enough calcium are subject to metabolic bone disease (MBD)—similar to rickets in humans. They are also *highly prone* to developing vitamin toxicity, also known as hypervitaminosis. Vitamin toxicity occurs when a treefrog consumes excessive amounts of vitamins (particularly vitamin A and D3). Vitamin toxicity causes lethargy, severe bloating or water edema, and irreversible kidney damage. Once vitamin toxicity has occurred, the damage is usually permanent, and the treefrog will almost certainly perish, as his internal organs may never function properly again. Avoid vitamin toxicity by supplementing your treefrog's diet no more than once each week.

Green treefrogs and most other species should be fed two or three times a week. Make sure each treefrog in your group gets his fair share.

Lightly dust one meal per week with two parts of calcium supplement powder to one part complete reptile vitamin/mineral supplement powder. In the case of younger specimens that are in a rapid phase of growth, supplementation may be more frequent: offer perhaps two dusted meals a week instead of one.

To dust feeder items, simply put a pinch of vitamin/mineral and calcium supplement powders in a small container and place several feeders inside as well. Close the container (a plastic bag or peanut butter jar both work great) and shake gently. When you place the prey items in your treefrog's terrarium, the powder will have adhered to their bodies, thereby lightly coating them in a thin layer of ghostly-white "dust."

Feeding Schedule

Maintain proper calcium/vitamin dosages and optimize your green treefrog's health by adhering to a strict feeding schedule. Young green treefrogs are in a stage of rapid growth and should be fed at least three to four times each week. Adult specimens may only require food twice each week. By placing a dish in the bottom of the terrarium from which prey cannot escape, you may leave several prey items in the terrarium so that your green treefrog may hunt and feed as he desires. Keeping a "feeding log" or journal with weekly entries will help you keep a handle on just how much your green treefrog is eating and how often he receives calcium/vitamin supplements.

Breeding Treefrogs

lthough green treefrogs are not terribly difficult to propagate in captivity, it is rarely ever done in large numbers. Green treefrogs are so populous in the wild and so inexpensive to purchase that captive breeding projects are simply too costly and too redundant to gain popularity among hobbyists. If, however, you are interested in breeding green treefrogs in captivity for reasons other than profit, then the news is good. Green treefrogs are prolific, stalwart animals whose reproductive cycle is easily stimulated under the right conditions. Once deposited, a green treefrog's eggs are easily hatched and the tadpoles easily reared into young froglets. Best of all, the entire process, from the mating of the parents to metamorphosis of the offspring, takes less than a season.

A blue variety of the green treefrog is occasionally seen in the wild, and breeders propagate them for the herp hobby.

Getting Started

Begin your breeding project by obtaining several pairs of green treefrogs. Since these treefrogs are semi-social animals, a single pair will not breed in isolation. In nature, males and females gather in large numbers and all mate at the same time. If this element of communal spawning is removed from the equation, then your chances of a successful breeding endeavor are slim. It is also important to understand the natural cycles of the environment your treefrogs come from and to try to simulate as best you can those conditions under which your treefrogs would normally mate. Since green treefrogs naturally spawn from March to October in the southern extremes of their range, and from April

Boys and Girls

Male green treefrogs are typically smaller than their female counterparts and sport dark, dirty-yellow throats. Females tend not only to be larger overall but also more rounded in appearance.

Cooling Concern

Remember that you should only cool down and breed green treefrogs that are healthy and in good weight. Green treefrogs that are not in prime condition may not survive the cool down.

to September in the northern reaches of their domain, it only makes sense to schedule your captive breeding project in synchrony with these months.

Around late October or early November, you'll want to begin conditioning your treefrogs for breeding in the following spring. Feed them heavily (more frequent meals, but without increasing their vitamin/mineral supplementation) until around mid-November. After they have had sufficient time to digest their last meals, cool their terrarium and decrease the amount of light they receive. Daily temperatures should not exceed 60 to 62°F, while nightly dips should not go below 54 to 56°F. Allow your treefrogs to receive no more than eight hours of daylight during this time period. If you have no living plants in the terrarium, I recommend against ever turning a light on directly over the terrarium. The ambient light shining in through your windows is plenty. The winter is also a time when green treefrogs—because they are hidden away in their winter retreats—are drier than at any other time of the year. Discontinue all misting of the terrarium, but do not allow your frogs to dry completely out. Maintain relative humidity of 55 to 60 percent.

Let It Rain

After a period of two months, return your green treefrogs to their normal temperature (mid-70s) and photoperiod, and resume feeding and misting them. Make sure that each treefrog is getting plenty to eat, as spawning will be physically taxing. Feed them well for three weeks, then place the pairs of treefrogs in a rain chamber.

Male treefrogs call to attract the females. Each species has a very specific call. The bird-voiced treefrog is named for the whistling call of the male.

A rain chamber is a special terrarium designed to encourage spawning behaviors. Construct a rain chamber by using a 20-gallon (or larger) glass aquarium fitted with a heavy-gauge screen lid. Into the bottom of the aquarium, place a fully submersible water pump, which you should be able to find at your local pet or gardening store. To the nozzle end of the pump (the expulsion nozzle), attach a sufficient length of plastic tubing. Run the tubing up the side of the terrarium and out through a small hole cut in the screen lid. Attach the end of the tubing to a section of PVC pipe (about three-quarters as long as the tank). Put a cap over one end of the PVC pipe and drill a number of small holes in a line down the length of the pipe. Let the PVC bar (called a spray bar) lay across the lid of the terrarium with its holes facing downward, into the terrarium.

Fill the terrarium with 3 to 6 inches of clean, chemical-free water, and turn on the pump. The pump will draw in water and push it through the tubing and into the PVC spray bar. Once inside the spray bar (which should only be about three-quarters as long as the terrarium), the water will "rain" back down into the terrarium, simulating a springtime shower. Once the water returns to the terrarium, it will be drawn into the pump once more to continue the shower within the totally self-contained rain chamber.

Because of the depth of the water inside the rain chamber, it is critical that you also put several perches or haul-outs in the chamber as well, for if they are without escape from the deep water, your treefrogs could easily tire and drown. One or two large pieces of driftwood work well for this purpose. Settle them on the base glass of the terrarium, and watch your treefrogs perch all over them during the showers.

Place your treefrogs into the rain chamber every night for several hours starting at sunset (for example, sunset until about 10 p.m., or your normal bedtime). Continue this for two weeks. Take care to change the water every night before putting your frogs into the rain chamber, as any wastes (feces, urine, etc.) excreted by your treefrogs into the chamber the night before can make for toxic, irritating rain that will soak through their skin and harm your treefrogs. Use fresh clean water every night.

Green treefrogs come down out of the trees to mate and lay their eggs in ponds and other still bodies of water.

Breeding Treefrogs

As additional breeding stimuli, you might consider using an audio loop tape of green treefrogs singing and chorusing in the wild. Simply go to an area populated by green treefrogs with a tape recorder and record about an hour's worth of chorusing. If you live in an area where this is not a practical option, you can easily download a sample of green treefrog singing from the Internet. The downloaded chorus will likely be much shorter than what you can record for yourself, but it will suffice. When you place your treefrogs in the rain chamber, simply play the tape (quite loudly) within earshot of your green treefrog pairs. The logic behind this practice is that your paired treefrogs will hear the recorded breeding calls, and will believe themselves to be amidst a great gathering of mating green treefrogs. I have experienced substantial success within my own breeding colonies by adding a loop tape of breeding choruses, and I highly recommend using such recordings.

Setting the Mood

Using a rain chamber and loop tapes of calling green treefrogs in conjunction with the treefrog's natural biological clock (i.e., attempting your breeding project in the spring when treefrogs naturally mate) will greatly increase the odds of success in your captive breeding endeavors.

Egg Laying

After a few nights of exposure to the rain chamber and the loop tapes, your treefrogs will likely begin breeding behavior. Excessive physical activity (jumping, swimming, walking) and prolonged chorusing are key indicators that breeding is imminent. When you see your green treefrogs engaging in odd-looking "wrestling matches," then you'll know your frogs are on the right track. Called *amplexus*, this behavior occurs when the male treefrog anchors himself on the female's back, gripping her under the forelimbs with his front legs. When he is firmly attached, and when she is ready, the couple will enter the water to spawn. She will begin kicking out strands of tiny, black eggs suspended in a jelly-like substance, and he will begin secreting sperm into the water directly atop the eggs. A large female green treefrog may deposit as many as 700 eggs in this manner. Once the eggs are fertilized, the male and female separate, but may spawn again, as many as two or three more times over the next week or so.

Once the eggs have been deposited, it is important that they develop in clean water, as foul water conditions will quickly destroy even the healthiest clutch of eggs. Maintain water conditions of 72 to 76°F with a slightly alkaline pH of 7.2 to 7.4. Eggs may be hatched and tadpoles reared in the rain chamber or moved to a separate tank outfitted with aged, chemically appropriate water. In either case, you should suspend a full-spectrum florescent bulb no less than one foot above the tank. In nature, tadpoles and their growth cycles are stimulated by direct sunlight, so a bright—though not overly warm—artificial sun should be used for at least 12 to 15 hours each day. Remember, the brightness of this hanging lamp is important, but the light *must not* significantly increase the water temperature. Don't hang the light too close over the aquarium.

Raising Tadpoles

Once tadpoles hatch, it is best to house them in aquaria at

Puzzled by pH?

If you have questions about controlling or monitoring the pH of your tadpole tank, check with your local pet store. They are likely to sell pH test kits and chemicals to control the pH. A good reptile- or fish-oriented store will also be able to offer advice on the issue.

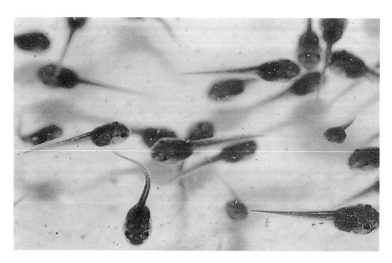

You can feed your tadpoles tropical fish flake, krill, freeze-dried worms, and other common fish foods. Cuban treefrog tadpoles are pictured here.

densities of no more than five tadpoles per gallon. When kept at higher densities, their wastes quickly pollute the water, and their voracious appetites may lead them to turn on one another. When food is scarce—both in captivity and in the wild—many tadpoles become cannibalistic. House tadpoles under similar water conditions as you housed the eggs: mid-70s (via a fully submersible heater) and pH of 7.2 to 7.4. The skin, gills, and bodily tissues of the developing tadpoles are highly sensitive to water chemistry. Acidic pH, spikes in ammonia, and high levels of nitrogenous gases are dangerous to the young tadpoles. As is true with the treefrog terrarium, the tadpole tank *must not* be covered by a glass lid, as an impermeable glass lid will trap in ammonia and other noxious gases.

Because superior water quality is so critical to the survival of the tadpole, I recommend employing a number of styles of filtration in the tadpole tank. To filter the water mechanically, use one (preferably two) air pump-driven foam filters. These filters contain no engines or moving parts to trap or injure the tadpole. Instead, they are powered by the physics of water displacement caused by rising air bubbles. The foam attachment on their end will collect solid debris (which will accumulate rapidly in the tadpole tank). As soon as the foam begins to look dirty, remove it for cleaning. A second, biological approach is also necessary. Add as many water hyacinth and water lettuce plants as you can. The root systems of these plants will act as powerful filters, removing and processing ammonia, nitrogen, and other harmful waste materials from the tank. Conduct weekly water changes of 25 percent in the tadpole tank, refilling the aquarium with aged or, ideally, charcoal-filtered water, making sure to match the temperature and pH of the new water with the water already in the tank.

Rear the young tadpoles on a diet of fish flakes, sinking fish tablets, bloodworms, krill, and other such finely ground foods. Because the developing tadpoles are in a rapid stage of development, they need all the nutrients they can get. Feed light to moderate meals two to three times each day, varying the diet as much as possible. Fish foods containing spirulina are especially important, and small amounts of spirulina-containing foods should be incorporated with every feeding.

Froglet Safety

If not supplied with ample escape routes or "haul-outs," metamorphosing froglets will exhaust themselves and drown in their aquarium. You can use live plants, driftwood, artificial plants, or rocks. Just be sure the young frogs can get up on them and out of the water.

As the tadpoles develop, they will grow larger and longer, and soon tiny legs will bud out at the base of the tail. After the back legs begin to grow, the tail will shrink and be reabsorbed into the body. Soon thereafter, the front legs will sprout and the gills will shrink. As soon as you see the beginnings of legs emerge, you must immediately outfit the aquarium with climbing areas and haul-

Breeding Treefrogs

Once your tadpoles develop their legs, they will need plants or other climbing areas so that they may leave the water.

outs onto which the newly metamorphosed froglets can perch. Young froglets who have lost their gills and cannot escape the water will soon exhaust themselves and drown. Excellent perches include plants such as water lettuce and water hyacinth, stands of driftwood, and large, flat stones seated on the base glass of the aquarium and rising to well above the water line. Remove the newly metamorphosed treefrogs to their own terrarium and rear them on appropriately sized crickets as discussed previously.

Quick & Easy Green Treefrog Care

Treefrog Health Care

There is good news and bad news when it comes to the diseases and disorders of the treefrogs. The good news is that compared to other reptile and amphibian pets, there are relatively fewer diseases and disorders that hylid treefrogs suffer from. Hardy animals with resilient immune systems, these frogs simply do not contract a wide variety of pathogens. The bad news, however, is that once a hylid treefrog does contract an ailment, the outcome is usually fatal for the amphibian. More good news comes in knowing that these fatalities usually occur not because the illness was incurable, but because the hobbyist was not aware of the problem until it was too late. Almost all diseases and disorders that afflict the treefrogs discussed in this book are curable, though some are easier to cure than others.

Finding a Herp Vet

It is not always easy to find vets who are experienced with reptiles and amphibians. Here are some suggestions to help you locate a vet who can help with your green treefrog. It is best if you locate one before you actually have an emergency

- Call veterinarians listed as "exotic" or "reptile" vets in the phonebook. Ask them questions to be sure they are familiar with green treefrogs.

- Ask at your local pet stores and animal shelters to see if there is someone they can recommend.

- Ask local zoos for a recommendation.

- Herpetological societies are likely to know which vets treat reptiles and amphibians.

- Contact the Association of Reptilian and Amphibian Veterinarians. Their website is www.arav.org.

By maintaining a close relationship with your herp veterinarian, taking your treefrogs in for medical treatment as soon as trouble signs arise, and by adhering to the strictest standards in husbandry and cleanliness, your pet treefrogs may live out their entire lives without ever suffering under the burden of disease. As you will see, virtually all treefrog ailments stem directly from poor hygiene in the terrarium. Maintaining sterile conditions in the terrarium is the first and most critical step in thwarting diseases and disorders before they occur. If your treefrog does fall ill, however, be sure to remove him to the quarantine terrarium, which will now act as a hospital tank. Maintain warm temperatures, proper humidity, and superior hygiene within the hospital tank so that your treefrog will make a speedy recovery.

Stress

Though some hobbyists do not consider stress to be a disease, I include it here as a "gateway disease," in that excessive stress opens the floodgates for other diseases. When humans are severely stressed—overworked, don't get enough sleep, don't eat right, etc.—we weaken our immune systems and open ourselves up to infections. The same is true of our little treefrog friends. The rigors of capture, shipping, transport, overcrowding at the distributor or in the pet shop, fluctuations in temperature, and the shock of moving from one geographic location to the next can seriously impact the immune system of wild-caught treefrogs. Even captive-bred individuals go through considerable unease when being shipped from the breeder to the pet shop and eventually on to your house. By having a warm, stable habitat set up and waiting for your new treefrog when he arrives, you can cut down greatly on his stress level.

Keeping that habitat warm, moist, and clean through the years will also guarantee that the treefrog's stress level stays as low as possible. Other factors that will increase a treefrog's stress are unsanitary living conditions, radical temperature swings, and improper diet. Once severe stress sets in, you can expect other, more virulent diseases to strike your treefrogs soon thereafter. Signs of stress include dark skin color, drying out of the skin, listlessness, and poor feeding habits.

Dehydration

When humidity conditions are less than suitable, most treefrogs can quickly become dehydrated (there are some species that have adapted to experience temporary severe dry periods). Symptoms of dehydration include a darkening of the colors (greens turn brown, grays darken significantly, etc.), wrinkling and drying out of the skin, closed eyes, and a total lack of movement. I guess the best way to describe it is that a dehydrated treefrog looks like he has been mummified: he is dry, creased, and ancient looking. Remedy by placing the dehydrated treefrog in a shallow pan of clean, fresh water. As the treefrog soaks (absorbing moisture back into his mummified body), you can sprinkle a few drops down the animal's back or gently spray him with a misting bottle every ten or fifteen minutes. This will help to hydrate the frog, while at the same time rinsing away any bits of substrate or clumped mucus that has dried onto his back. Dehydration among captive treefrogs is a key sign that something is wrong in your terrarium. Either your humidity level is too low, your heating lamp is of too high a wattage, or all the water has evaporated from the substrate. Remedy by switching to a lower wattage bulb or raising the relative humidity inside the terrarium.

Escapee treefrogs often suffer from dehydration as well. Found on the carpet the next day, an escaped green treefrog will appear as a slowly moving clump of hair or carpet fibers. Again, place the frog in a shallow dish of water and mist him periodically, taking care to remove any and all debris clinging to his body.

Bacterial Infections

Bacteria are opportunistic pathogens that are normally warded off by the immune systems of healthy treefrogs. Once your animals become severely stressed, however, bacteria are quick to strike. The most common pathogens are *Pseudomonas*, which manifest through suddenly appearing sores, lesions, and unexplained, festering wounds. The appearance of such wounds warrants an immediate trip to the veterinarian, where the wounds will be swabbed, cultured, and properly diagnosed for treatment. Because green treefrogs and their kin are so sensitive to medication, no treatment should be offered without veterinary supervision. Bacterial treatments may include subcutaneous injections or medicated sprays, which will be absorbed through the treefrog's semi-permeable skin.

Injuries

Occasionally, a treefrog may sustain injuries or sores that do not

Red-Leg

Perhaps the most well-known and feared of all frog ailments is red-leg disease, which is brought about by prolonged exposure to unsanitary conditions, cold temperatures, excessive moisture, etc. As the disease's name suggests, symptoms include a red rash or reddish discoloration forming under the thighs and toe pads of the hind legs, as well as on the belly. This redness is the result of internal hemorrhaging of subcutaneous capillaries caused by an opportunistic bacterial infection. Other symptoms include listlessness, lack of appetite, bloating, and general malaise. Tetracycline is often effective, but you should consult a veterinarian for successful treatment. Avoid future outbreaks of red-leg by maintaining warm, sanitary conditions and proper levels of relative humidity.

stem from bacterial infection. Animals may be banged about, rubbed raw, or otherwise abraded during transport. Nonbacterial wounds that are not promptly treated are virtually guaranteed to become infected and worsen. Severe wounds warrant immediate veterinary attention. Remember to not administer any drug to your treefrog without first consulting a herp-specific veterinarian for proper diagnosis and treatment dosages and schedule, as overmedicating a green treefrog (or any treefrog, for that matter) can be as deadly than the ailment from which he suffers.

Internal Parasites

Unexplained and sudden weight loss, runny feces, and general listlessness are all symptoms that your treefrog is suffering from internal parasites. Fortunately, internal parasites rarely afflict the treefrogs discussed in this book, and they are more commonly associated with imported tropical specimens. Internal parasites come in two forms, the nematodes and the protozoans. Nematodes are worms that digest much of the nutrients that your treefrog consumes. So a frog that eats and eats while constantly losing

All wild-caught treefrogs are likely to be carrying internal parasites. Follow your veterinarian's instructions for successful treatment of this problem.

weight is likely to be infected by nematodes. Treefrogs whose stool is runny or bloody are likely the hosts of a protozoan infection, though a fecal exam by your vet will be necessary for a definite diagnosis. If you suspect your treefrog to have internal parasites, take him to the vet immediately for diagnosis and treatment. Both nematodes and protozoa can be effectively routed by oral dosages of fenbendazole or metronidazole, which your veterinarian will prescribe.

Cloudy Eye

Recently imported treefrogs that have suffered eye injuries make up the lion's share of cloudy eye cases. These unlucky individuals may have been poked, struck, or even bitten (by another frog) in the eye. Immune system failure will also lead to cloudy eyes. If you are inspecting a potential pet treefrog and you see that his eyes look cloudy, whitish, bluish, or smoky, do not purchase him.

Quick & Easy Green Treefrog Care

Another cause of cloudy eye is unsanitary water conditions. If your treefrog is continually subjected to standing pools of filthy water, then he will likely absorb ammonia and other impurities into his body and subsequently display tainted or cloudy eyes. Treat by clearing the terrarium of its foul-water pools, and allow your treefrog to soak in a shallow dish (no more than half the frog's resting height) of clean, pure water. As the clean water soaks through the treefrog's skin, the impurities in his bloodstream will be diluted and expelled from his body. Repeat clean water soaks until the cloudiness disappears, and visit a vet if the problem does not resolve quickly.

Metabolic Bone Disease

Metabolic bone disease (MBD) is a condition in which the afflicted treefrog has gone for too long without receiving sufficient amounts of calcium or vitamin D in his diet. MBD causes the bones to become soft, frail, and flexible, and the frog stops moving, jumping, and feeding as he would naturally. Symptoms of MBD include sagging jaws, perpetually open mouth, sprawled hind legs, and inability to feed. If caught early, MBD is treatable under veterinary care. Dietary supplements of bird hand-feeding formula administered directly into the treefrog's stomach via a syringe may be necessary. After your veterinarian has diagnosed MBD and instructed proper treatment, the treefrog should recover fully and live the rest of his life as normal. Remember to prevent MBD simply by providing the correct, healthy amounts of calcium your pet needs.

Edema or Bloating

Characterized by swollen limbs and a chunky, bloated appearance, edema is a condition in which the treefrog's body is retaining excessive amounts of water. Edema generally has two causes. If it is caused by kidney failure due to vitamin toxicity, edema all too often proves fatal. If, however, the edema is brought on by unsanitary husbandry practices and infrequent terrarium cleanings, then it may be remedied. Because a treefrog's skin is semi-permeable, any toxins or contaminants contained in the terrarium's water column will affect the treefrog's internal systems. Feces, urine, rotting insect carcasses, and other biological wastes left in the terrarium will emit noxious vapors as they fester and rot. These vapors will become trapped in the humid terrarium; the evaporating water accumulating dangerously high levels of ammonia and nitrogen from the rotting wastes. Once this water settles back on the terrarium glass, the treefrog will begin to soak the biological impurities back into his system.

If your treefrog shows symptoms of toxic edema (bloating, twitching, eye cloudiness, general dullness of color), then soak the treefrog in a shallow pan of *clean* water for several hours. The clean, fresh water will soak into the frog's system and dilute the toxins in his bloodstream. Avoid edema by limiting vitamin supplements to once each week, and by maintaining clean, sanitary conditions inside your treefrog's terrarium.

Common Treefrog Species

The green treefrog certainly isn't the only member of the genus *Hyla* that makes an excellent pet. There are numerous other hylids that can be greatly rewarding and interesting captives. While there isn't room to list them all here, I have included some of the most popular and rewarding hylids that are frequently sold in pet shops and kept in captivity. Most of these are North American natives.

Green Treefrog, *Hyla cinerea*
Size: 1.75 to 2.5 inches.
Description: As their common name suggests, this species is the greenest of all North American treefrogs. Dorsal coloration ranges

Green treefrogs are often brown when cold, dry, or sleeping. If yours stays brown for any length of time, you should make sure your cage conditions are adequate.

from hunter to emerald green. Golden circles, ringed in black, are present atop the head, back, and thighs among certain populations, while a thick, whitish to pale-yellow stripe runs from the lips to the hind legs. The skin is smooth, and the iris of the eye is golden to burnt orange.

Longevity: Three to six years.

Sexing: Males of the species are typically smaller than their female counterparts, and sport dark, dirty-yellow throats.

Breeding: After being cooled for two to three months at temperatures of 57 to 62°F, raise the temps to 70 to 74°F and introduce your green treefrogs to one another (at least two males and three females) in a rain chamber during mid-March to May. Expose to rain showers in the chamber for several nights in a row. These showers will coax your animals into mating, particularly if the showers occur in conjunction with a front of low barometric pressure. Amplexus usually occurs at night. Females will deposit up to 700 eggs. Tadpoles metamorphose in four to six weeks. Females may deposit more than one clutch of eggs per season.

Special Care: A highly visible species, the green treefrog may sit in the open during the daytime. Plenty of wide, smooth perches (especially broad-leafed plants and wide stems and branches) will accommodate this frog's diurnal activities.

Pet Suitability: Hardy and easily cared for, the green treefrog is a beginner's best choice for a pet treefrog. Very active at night, these frogs are rarely afraid to present themselves during the daytime as well, thereby making them highly attractive and highly visible terrarium inhabitants. A green treefrog's hearty appetite and willingness to feed in captivity helps to ensure his survival in the terrarium. Be warned, however, that green treefrogs may become raucous when a low-pressure front moves through, singing their loud *quank, quank, quank* song at night.

Barking Treefrog, *Hyla gratiosa*

Size: 2 to 2.75 inches.

Description: An attractive treefrog, this large amphibian is of stocky build and highly variable coloration. Dorsal coloration ranges from solid olive green to emerald with circular black spots. In addition to these spots, some individuals also bear whitish to cream colored speckles. The upper lip is barred in white to pinkish, as is the top side of the hind feet. The skin of the barking treefrog is dimpled in scores of tiny bumps, giving him a much rougher texture than his green treefrog cousin. As his common name suggests, the barking treefrog's call is a short, gruff *raaarrkk, raaarrkk*, which sounds much like a barking dog. During the mating season, however, this animal emits a crisp, clear, bell-tone note.

Barking treefrogs breed at roughly the same time as the green treefrogs. The care of the eggs and tadpoles of the two species is the same.

Longevity: If kept in good health, the barking treefrog is perhaps the longest-lived of all North American treefrogs; captive life spans often exceed seven years.

Sexing: Mature males of the species have a loose, pale greenish to yellow throat.

Breeding: Barking treefrogs must be cooled to 58 to 62°F for at least two months prior to mating. Introduce at least two males with an equal number of females. Mates from March to August. Mating habits and tadpole-rearing tactics are as described for the green treefrog.

Special Care: During the summer months, wild barking treefrogs may burrow into the soil to escape the searing summer heat. Captive specimens may also wish to burrow into the substrate of your terrarium. To accommodate this natural behavior, be sure to include plenty of ground-level hides in the terrarium, and employ moist (peat moss) substrate that is at least three inches deep.

Captive Diet: Mealworms (superworms), crickets, wax worms, maggots.

Pet Suitability: Docile, hardy, and infinitely attractive, the barking treefrog may also be the most personable of all the North American treefrogs. Specimens tolerate short periods of gentle handling, and can become so tame that they will readily accept food from their keeper's fingers! This species can be kept communally with other species or with others of their own kind, provided all frogs are of similar size.

Gray Treefrog, *Hyla versicolor* / Cope's Treefrog, *Hyla chrysoscelis*

Size: 1.5 to 2.5 inches.

Description: Small, quietly attractive treefrogs, the gray and Cope's treefrogs are visually indistinguishable from one another; thus I group them together here. Both species wear a dorsal coat of charcoal gray to mossy green with marbled white and leaden hues, giving them the appearance of lichen or tree bark. The inside edges of the hind legs are painted in brilliant yellow, orange, and red splotches, while a dark-edged light patch is present directly under

It is impossible to distinguish gray treefrogs from Cope's treefrogs without hearing their calls or examining their chromosomes in a laboratory.

the eye. The skin is granular and rough, and the call is a resonating, rasping trill.

Longevity: Three to four years is common.

Sexing: Males of the species have a dark yellow throat.

Breeding: After a four to ten week cooling period at 48 to 55°F, males and females will readily mate under the same conditions as described for the green treefrog.

Special Care: Frequently kept in small colonies. Gray and Cope's treefrogs are arboreal creatures who spend virtually all of their time in the treetops. Thus, captive specimens need retreats that are situated very high in the terrarium to accommodate their lofty lifestyle.

Captive Diet: Small mealworms, crickets, and maggots.

Pet Suitability: Gray and Cope's treefrogs are not the most personable of species and may resent even the gentlest handling. They do, however, thrive in captivity, and can make excellent subjects of observation. Because of their benign nature, one or more Cope's or gray treefrogs can make interesting additions to elaborate, living vivariums that already contain other treefrog species. When housed together, these treefrogs can become quite vocal in the deep hours of the night.

Common Treefrog Species

Pacific Treefrog, *Hyla regilla*

Pacific treefrogs are highly variable in color. Individuals may be green, brown, reddish brown, gray, or tan.

Size: Up to 2 inches.

Description: One of North America's most well-known treefrogs, this demure creature is the amphibian of choice for Hollywood directors desiring a natural sounding night-time setting. Recordings of this frog's shrill, musical voice have been heard by moviegoers for over half a century. Wearing a base coat of lime green to light tan or even black, the Pacific treefrog is recognizable by a dark brown to black stripe running from the upper lip, between the nostrils and eyes, and ending just above the forelimbs. The dorsal surface is often mottled in dark blotches, while the flanks bear roundish spots or dark ocelli. The skin is rough, dimpled with knobs and protuberances of varying sizes.

Longevity: Pacific treefrogs are not noted for their longevity, which rarely exceeds two and a half years in captivity.

Sexing: The male Pacific treefrog has a charcoal to leaden throat pouch, while the female's throat is whitish to tan.

Breeding: Captive breeding of the Pacific treefrog is not easily accomplished outside of this animal's natural range, as elevation and climatic changes, which are key to successful mating, are difficult to simulate. Mating occurs from January to August, and may occur during periods of cool temperatures (55 to 65°F).

Special Care: In the wild, the Pacific treefrog is frequently encountered on the ground or in very low-growing bushes. It flourishes in low, wide terrariums, and may never venture more than a few feet off the ground. Outfit this species' terrarium with thick, moist substrate and plenty of low cover: short plants, low-growing foliage, ferns, etc. Pacific treefrogs also require cooler temperatures

Treefrog Communities

Green, gray (Cope's), barking, and squirrel treefrogs are communal animals that will thrive if housed together in a community terrarium. When housing multiple treefrogs in the same enclosure, make sure each receives plenty of food and has ample retreats. Each treefrog should be similar in size to prevent them from feeding on each other.

than their green cousins; daily highs need not exceed the mid- to upper 70s.

Captive Diet: Pinhead crickets, very small mealworms, wax worms, and maggots.

Pet Suitability: While he is not overly difficult to care for, the Pacific treefrog is better suited to those hobbyists who already have some experience in dealing with treefrogs. Because of his small stature, this animal is one of the more fragile treefrogs and should not be handled unnecessarily. So far as ornamental value and beauty goes, however, a terrarium hosting a small colony of Pacific treefrogs is hard to beat. Many hobbyists find the musical notes of this frog's chorus, which is reminiscent of distant tolling bells, particularly pleasing to the ear.

Squirrel Treefrog, *Hyla squirella*

Size: 1 to 1.75 inches.

Description: Even in adulthood, this is a very small treefrog. Body coloration ranges from brownish to green, with poorly defined whitish to tan stripes along the upper jaw and each flank. Body stripes may be absent in some populations. Small speckles may or may not be present along the back and thighs. The center of back is usually the darkest portion, with color lightening toward the sides. Belly is cream to yellowish. Enlarged toe pads.

Longevity: Two to three years is common.

Sexing: Males have bright yellow throats and are typically smaller than females.

The squirrel treefrog is a very small treefrog. Be careful housing this species with larger frogs, or the squirrel treefrog may become lunch.

Breeding: Mating occurs in early spring after a two to three month cooling period. Frogs of both sexes gather in grasses, weed clusters, and in other low-growing vegetation bordering seasonal ponds and flooded ditches. Females deposit up to 1,000 eggs. Tadpoles metamorphose in 40 to 50 days.

Special Care: If housed together in colonies, this species benefits from large, horizontally or vertically oriented hides. In nature, over a dozen squirrel treefrogs may congregate in communal hideaways, thus similar retreats should be offered in captivity. This species particularly relishes artificial vines in the home terrarium. Suitable hides are easily constructed from plywood, cork bark, or even opaque plastic.

Captive Diet: Crickets, mealworms, wax worms, and other small insects offered after dark.

Pet Suitability: Squirrel treefrogs, like their larger green cousins, make excellent starter treefrogs and are well suited for the novice hobbyist. These treefrogs may be shy about accepting food during the daylight hours. Any coyness in these animals almost certainly disappears with the setting of the sun, and the normally shy frogs will become ravenous predators.

Bird-Voiced Treefrog, *Hyla avivoca*

Size: 1.75 to 2.25 inches.

Description: Greenish to grayish brown with darker chocolate blotches adorning the back, head, and hind limbs, the bird-voiced treefrog is also recognizable by the presence of a dark-rimmed yellowish to greenish spot directly beneath the eye. Like his gray cousin, the bird-voiced treefrog has vibrantly colored patches along the inner thigh. Visible only when the frog hops or leaps, these patches range from pale lime green to a deep emerald hue.

Longevity: Two to four years.

Sexing: Males of the species are considerably smaller than the females, and during the spring of the year, males' throats darken considerably.

Breeding: Breeds from March to September. Large numbers of males gather in branches and weeds overhanging a quiet pool of water, while masses of females gather at the water's edge below. In captivity, cool your frogs for six to eight weeks at 54 to 58°F. Females may deposit several hundred eggs. Tadpoles metamorphose in 45 to 50 days.

Special Care: During the daylight hours, the bird-voiced treefrog takes refuge high in the forest canopy. Because of his propensity for heights, the bird-voiced treefrog needs perhaps the tallest terrarium of all the treefrogs. Outfit the terrarium with vertical climbing branches ending in dense clusters of artificial vegetation at their uppermost reaches. In the wild, the bird-voiced treefrog thrives in trees and shrubs that grow in standing water. This species does best, therefore, when the terrarium is outfitted with lots of standing water in the bottom. This can be achieved either by filling several wide, but shallow dishes, and changing the water every couple of days, or by constructing one big pool of living, circulating aquarium water in

The bird-voiced treefrog and the gray treefrog can be hard to tell apart. On the bird-voiced, the colored patches on the back legs are greenish to yellowish, not orange as in the gray treefrog.

the bottom of the terrarium. In either case, stones, branches, and artificial plants should extend into the water to act as escape routes should your treefrog fall into the water.

Captive Diet: Small crickets, mealworms, wax worms, and maggots.

Pet Suitability: There are two major drawbacks to keeping the bird-voiced treefrog in captivity. The first is that—unlike their green treefrog cousin—this highly reclusive species seldom presents itself during the daytime, and will likely never be seen in the open when the terrarium is lit. Secondly, the bird-voiced treefrog produces skin secretions that are mildly toxic and may cause sneezing, runny nose, watery eyes, and other allergy-symptoms to those who handle him. For most hobbyists, however, this treefrog's magnificent voice more than makes up for any drawbacks associated with his husbandry. When he calls, the bird-voiced treefrog emits a very musical, airy series of whistles that sound much like the song of a bird.

Cuban Treefrog, *Osteopilus septentrionalis*

Size: 2.5 to 5.25 inches

Description: Although it is not a member of the genus *Hyla*, the Cuban treefrog is so frequently encountered in pet shops and reptile

One of the most common frogs sold in pet shops is the Cuban treefrog. It is large and hardy, making a good pet.

Mixed Species

Given their small size and easy care, many treefrogs lend themselves well to naturalistic enclosures with a mix of other herps. If you decide to mix in some other animals, there are a few guidelines to follow. First, all of the animals must have similar care requirements. Second, all should be of similar size to prevent them from eating each other or out-competing each other for food. Third, the keeper must be prepared to separate the animals should the mixing not work out.

The following is a list of some species that should do well in a terrarium with some treefrogs. There may be others that will work, also. You should research each species' requirements before you decide to add it to your treefrog habitat.

Brown Anole, *Anolis sagrei*
Fire-bellied Toad, *Bombina orientalis* (requires a swimming area)
Green Anole, *Anolis carolinensis*
House Gecko, *Hemidactylus frenatus*

web sites that I include the species here. Unwittingly introduced to southern Florida in the early 1950s, this animal is the largest treefrog found in North America. The highly variable coloration ranges from mottled brown, bronze, olive green, tan, or even a light lead gray. The hind legs are frequently barred in alternating bands of lighter and darker coloration. This species also bears enormous toe pads and broad skull and jawbones. Irises are golden to bright yellow.

Longevity: Two to four years.

Sexing: Females are by far the larger of the two sexes. Males seldom exceed 2.5 inches long.

Breeding: Very prolific breeders, Cuban treefrogs will come into season after a brief winter cooling period of 65 to 69°F for three to seven weeks. Under conditions of warm days, slightly cooler nights, high humidity, and low barometric pressure, members of each sex will congregate to breed. Females deposit strings of 1,200 to over 2,000 eggs. Tadpoles hatch in 24 to 72 hours, and may be fed on flake fish food. Tadpoles metamorphose in six to nine weeks and attain sexual maturity in 10 to 12 months.

Special Care: Due to this species' voracious appetite and highly predatory nature, these frogs *absolutely must* be housed individually. Mixing a Cuban treefrog with other species or even others of his own kind will result in the largest animal eventually attacking and devouring all his tankmates. Daily temperatures should be kept in the upper 70s to low 80s, with dips into the mid-70s at night. Prefers broad-leafed plants such as palms and elephant ear.

Captive Diet: Mealworms (superworms), wax worms, crickets, and maggots. Large adults will also accept goldfish and pinkie mice.

Pet Suitability: If housed alone, Cuban treefrogs can make interesting pets. Take care when handling, however, as these powerful leapers have a propensity for escape, and once loose in your house, they will quickly seek dark cover, disappearing behind heavy furniture or into an air duct in a matter of seconds. Escapees can usually be recaptured at night near sinks, toilets, dishwashers, or other sources of water. Note that Cuban treefrogs secrete noxious mucus from their skin, which can be irritating to a keeper's eyes, nostrils, and skin. Always wash your hands immediately after handling a Cuban treefrog.

Resources

MAGAZINES

Contemporary Herpetology
Southeastern Louisiana University
www.nhm.ac.uk/hosted_sites/ch

Herp Digest
www.herpdigest.org

Reptiles Magazine
P.O. Box 6050
Mission Viejo, CA 92690
www.animalnetwork.com/reptiles

ORGANIZATIONS

American Society of Ichthyologists and Herpetologists
Maureen Donnelly, Secretary
Grice Marine Laboratory
Florida International University
Biological Sciences
11200 SW 8th St.
Miami, FL 33199
Telephone: (305) 348-1235
E-mail: asih@fiu.edu
www.asih.org

Amphibian, Reptile & Insect Association
Liz Price
23 Windmill Rd
Irthlingsborough
Wellingborough NN9 5RJ
England

Society for the Study of Amphibians and Reptiles (SSAR)
Marion Preest, Secretary
The Claremont Colleges
925 N. Mills Ave.
Claremont, CA 91711
Phone: 909-607-8014
E-mail: mpreest@jsd.claremont.edu
www.ssarherps.org

List of Local Herp Societies
www.kingsnake.com/society.html

WEB RESOURCES

Frogdaze
www.frogdaze.com

Frog Directory
www.frogdirectory.com

Frogland
www.allaboutfrogs.org

Frog Watch USA
www.frogwatch.org

HerpNetwork
www.herpnetwork.com

Living Under World
www.livingunderworld.org

VETERINARY RESOURCES

Association of Reptile and Amphibian Veterinarians
P.O. Box 605
Chester Heights, PA 19017
Phone: 610-358-9530
Fax: 610-892-4813
E-mail: ARAVETS@aol.com
www.arav.org

RESCUE AND ADOPTION SERVICES

ASPCA
424 East 92nd Street
New York, NY 10128-6801
Phone: (212) 876-7700
E-mail: information@aspca.org
www.aspca.org

Petfinder.org
www.petfinder.org

RSPCA (UK)
Wilberforce Way
Southwater
Horsham, West Sussex RH13 9RS
Telephone: 0870 3335 999
www.rspca.org.uk

Index

Measurement Conversion Chart

UNITS USED IN THIS BOOK

1 gallon = 3.7854 liters
1 inch = 2.54 centimeters
32°F = 0°C (water freezes)
75°F = 23.9°C

CONVERTING FAHRENHEIT TO CELSIUS

Subtract 32 from the Fahrenheit temperature.
Divide the answer by 9.
Multiply that answer by 5.

Photo Credits

R. D. Babb: 37, 53
Marian Bacon: 4
R. D. Bartlett: 33, 40, 42
I. Francais: 10, 24
Paul Freed: 34, 52
James E. Gerholdt: 11, 48, 51, 55
Barry Mansell: 18, 36, 43
W. P. Mara: 14
Sean McKeown: 56
G. & C. Merker: 1, 13
A. Norman: 59
Philip Purser: 5, 7, 22
M. Smith: 26
Michael Smoker: 25
K. H. Switak: 3, 31, 58, 60